Original title:
Whispers of Ice

Copyright © 2024 Swan Charm
All rights reserved.

Author: Liina Liblikas
ISBN HARDBACK: 978-9908-52-053-7
ISBN PAPERBACK: 978-9908-52-054-4
ISBN EBOOK: 978-9908-52-055-1

Ghostly Frost Dances

In the quiet night, they sway and glide,
Whispers of chill that the winds confide.
Moonlit patterns upon the ground,
With every step, a soft sound found.

Wraiths of ice in swirling flight,
Frosty tendrils in pale moonlight.
A delicate brush paints the trees,
Bowing softly to the chilly breeze.

Each breath a plume, a vapor trace,
Nature's artistry, a fleeting grace.
Silver shimmers on the frozen lake,
Glistening visions that the night makes.

Time stands still in this frigid domain,
Echoes of laughter, joy intertwined with pain.
Specters dance, both gentle and stark,
Living harmonies in the frosty dark.

As dawn breaks, the shadows retreat,
Leaving only remnants of a frost-kissed sheet.
Yet in the heart, the chill remains,
A memory of the ghostly refrains.

Beneath the Still White Canopy

Under the arch of winter's embrace,
A white blanket rests, a tranquil space.
Silent whispers in the frosty air,
Cold dreams linger, drifting everywhere.

Trees stand proud, cloaked in snow,
Wonders of winter in a soft glow.
Footprints marked in the blanket bright,
Guide our journey through the night.

Stars twinkle down from their throne,
Glistening jewels on the frost-stitched stone.
A hush envelops all that is near,
Nature breathes soft, a world sincere.

As shadows stretch in fading light,
We wander through this serene night.
Under the stillness, secrets are spun,
Life whispers softly, a promise begun.

Yet as dawn graces the frozen crest,
The beauty of night puts dreams to rest.
Beneath the canopy, peace remains,
In every heartbeat, the stillness gains.

Silent Crystals

Delicate forms in the morning dew,
Silent crystals glisten, a jeweled view.
Nature's artwork, intricate design,
Captured light in each shard so fine.

Frost-kissed petals, soft and rare,
A fleeting beauty, beyond compare.
Each breath a moment, pure and clear,
Whispering secrets to those who hear.

Scattered jewels on the surface wide,
Reflecting wonders where shadows hide.
In this stillness, the world stands still,
Crystals singing, a gentle thrill.

Caught in a web of shimmering lace,
Time slips by in an endless grace.
With every sparkle, a story is told,
Of moments cherished, forever bold.

As twilight falls, they start to fade,
Silent crystals in the evening shade.
Yet in the heart, their memory lies,
A treasure hidden beneath the skies.

Chilling Echoes

In the frozen air, a sound so sweet,
Chilling echoes call from the earth beneath.
Crystals shatter in the morning light,
A haunting song that dances in flight.

Winds weave tales of those long gone,
In whispers soft as the breaking dawn.
Nature's chorus, ethereal and frail,
Guiding hearts with their gentle trail.

Each note a sigh, a fleeting air,
Echoing stories of love and despair.
Embrace the chill, let it enfold,
In every echo, a secret told.

Footfalls linger on the frosty land,
Memories etched like footprints in sand.
Listen closely, the echoes grow,
Bringing forth feelings we all know.

As daylight fades, the chill arrives,
In echoes lived, our spirit survives.
Haunted yet whole, we rise and roam,
Carried by echoes that lead us home.

Beneath the Icebound Sky

Underneath the frozen glow,
Stars are silent, signs below.
Whispers float on chilly air,
Dreams are caught in winter's snare.

Moonlight dances on the lake,
Shadows flicker, wishes wake.
Nature's breath, a tender sigh,
Secrets held beneath the sky.

Crystals blink in frosty night,
Every glance a fleeting light.
Beneath it all, a heartbeat slow,
Life awaits the thawing show.

Echoes of a world concealed,
In the silence, truths revealed.
Hope lies buried, waiting still,
For the warmth to come and fill.

Through the icebound, dreams will soar,
Beneath the sky, forevermore.
A tapestry of dusk and dawn,
In winter's grip, we carry on.

Glistening Whispers of Winter

Snowflakes dance on silver trails,
Glistening whispers weave their tales.
Breathe the air, a crisp delight,
Wrapped in wonder, pure as white.

Branches draped in frosted dreams,
Moonlit glows like childhood schemes.
Every step, a crunch below,
Footprints in the hush of snow.

Fires crackle, warmth ignites,
Stories shared on winter nights.
Hot cocoa warms the chilly hands,
Happy laughter ever stands.

Windows framed by icy lace,
Tender hearts find their embrace.
In this realm of soft repose,
Magic blooms where winter goes.

Glistening whispers, sweet and clear,
Transforming all that we hold dear.
As the season unfolds anew,
In winter's song, we find our cue.

Silent Reverberations of the North

In the north, the silence hums,
A symphony of stillness drummed.
Frosted waves upon the air,
Whispers float without a care.

Mountains bow to the pale light,
Veils of snow in purest white.
Nature holds its breath and waits,
For the sun to change the fates.

Echoes linger in the pines,
Secrets held in tangled vines.
Every moment, crisp and clear,
Winter's voice draws ever near.

Footfalls soft on winter's coat,
Thoughts adrift, they gently float.
Radiant calm, a perfect peace,
In this realm, all troubles cease.

Silent reverberations blend,
A quiet magic will not end.
Northward winds bring stories told,
In every flake, a dream unfolds.

Memories in a Snowdrift

In a snowdrift, dreams arise,
Soft and white like gentle sighs.
Captured moments drift away,
Whispers from the fading day.

Childhood laughter fills the air,
Memories spun with tender care.
Snowball fights and sledding thrill,
Echo on the winter's chill.

Frozen tales on frosty ground,
In each flake, a joy is found.
Winter's canvas, pure and bright,
Paints the world in sparkling white.

Days grow short and nights are long,
In these moments, we belong.
Each breath held in a snow-draped hour,
Time stands still, a precious power.

Memories in snowdrifts lie,
Storing laughter, love, and sighs.
In the depths of winter's breath,
We find life's warmth, beyond the death.

Tundra's Heart

In the silence, the winds do roam,
Whispers of ice, a chilling home.
Nature's canvas, vast and wide,
Secrets burrowed deep inside.

Crystals glisten in the pale light,
A tranquil world, frozen yet bright.
Footprints trace where shadows play,
In the heart of the tundra's sway.

Beneath the veil of the starry night,
The northern lights dance, a wondrous sight.
In solitude, the heart beats slow,
A rhythm felt in the falling snow.

Ethereal beauty, the landscape sings,
In winter's hold, the spirit clings.
Every breath, a cloud in the air,
A moment captured, fragile and rare.

Life persists in a frozen embrace,
In this vast, wild, and distant place.
The tundra whispers, stories untold,
Of starry nights and hearts of cold.

Frosty Reveries

In dreams of frost, the twilight calls,
Snowflakes tumble, the silence falls.
A blanket white, the world in peace,
Where every worry finds release.

Glistening branches, a lacy design,
Nature's art, a moment divine.
With winter's breath, the air turns still,
A serene beauty, beyond the hill.

Under the stars, the night unfurls,
Whispers of magic in frozen swirls.
The moonlight dances on icy streams,
A realm of wonder, where hope redeems.

In frosty reveries, dreams take flight,
Through jagged peaks in the dead of night.
Nature's lullaby, soft and sweet,
In winter's hush, our hearts will meet.

With every step on the powdery ground,
Life's sweetest secrets can be found.
In a world adorned with shimmering grace,
Where winter holds its warm embrace.

Icy Serenade

An icy serenade, the winter's song,
Echoes softly, where shadows belong.
In the stillness, the world seems to pause,
Nature's beauty, deserving applause.

Frost-kissed valleys, in silver repose,
A magical sight where the cold wind blows.
The trees adorned in crystal attire,
A fairytale landscape, our hearts inspire.

Winds whisper tales of days gone by,
Beneath the vast and silent sky.
Each flake that falls, a story to tell,
In the heart of winter, we dwell.

Through frosty nights, a journey awaits,
In shimmering worlds, where time abates.
Listen closely, let the heart be swayed,
By the beauty of life in an icy serenade.

As dawn breaks gently, the colors ignite,
Golds and pinks chase away the night.
Hope is reborn in the warming light,
In winter's embrace, everything feels right.

Shadows in the Snow

Footprints vanish, hidden from view,
In shadows cloaked, where silence grew.
The world wraps tight in layers of white,
A canvas untouched, bathed in light.

Shadows whisper as the night descends,
In frosty quiet, the journey bends.
Beneath the stars, the secrets are sown,
In the softest blanket of glimmering snow.

Trees stand tall, their branches bare,
Guardians of stories that dance in the air.
Each sparkling flake, a wish from the past,
In the rising wind, those moments last.

The moonlight casts a gentle glow,
Illuminating paths in the drifts below.
A lullaby sung by the wind at play,
Guiding lost souls, showing the way.

As dawn unfolds, the shadows take flight,
Embraced by warmth, chasing the night.
In the snow, we wish, we dream, we flow,
Finding our peace in the shadows of snow.

Beneath the Icy Veil

Beneath the icy veil, we tread,
Whispers of frost kiss the earth,
Stars glimmer softly overhead,
In silence, nature shows its worth.

Frozen breath dances on the air,
Crystal branches sway and creak,
The world holds secrets, hidden, rare,
In the hush, it begins to speak.

A blanket of snow cloaks the ground,
Footsteps muffled, lost in night,
Every heart, a stirring sound,
In the stillness, we find delight.

Hushed dreams linger with the cold,
Each flake a tale from the skies,
Nature's beauty, a treasure untold,
Beneath the veil, the spirit flies.

Nighttime blankets all in white,
Glowing moon, our only guide,
Beneath the stars, pure and bright,
In the chilly peace, we bide.

Encased in Silence

Encased in silence, shadows loom,
The night enfolds like a soft sigh,
In the stillness, hears the gloom,
Whispers echo, as time slips by.

Each snowflake falls, a gentle sound,
Resting softly on the ground,
In this quiet, lost and found,
Peace unwinds, a novel bound.

Frosty breath on a window pane,
The world outside, a canvas white,
Every thought a fleeting grain,
Images captured in the night.

Stars blink out, their stories told,
Overhead, a celestial light,
In the beauty, hearts unfold,
Encased in silence, we ignite.

Amid the quiet, we can roam,
Finding solace in the chill,
Wandering far from hearth and home,
In silence wrapped, we're standing still.

Shiver of the Cold Night

A shiver dances in the night,
Wrapped in layers, warm and tight,
Moonbeams glisten on pure snow,
Casting shadows, soft and slow.

The chill bites at my fingertips,
Breath condenses, clouds arise,
Whispers travel on the lips,
Of frosty winds beneath the skies.

Branches sway with icy grace,
Nature's beauty, sharp and bright,
Every glance a fleeting trace,
Of memories held in the night.

Stars twinkle like distant dreams,
In this wonder, we embrace,
Silent glimmers, soft moonbeams,
Lead us through the shadowed space.

As the night grows ever deep,
In the chill, we find our way,
Nature's hold, both firm and steep,
In the freeze, we long to stay.

Glacial Echoes in the Dark

In the dark, glacial echoes call,
Whispers of ice in the night,
Nature pauses, shadows fall,
Every breath a fleeting light.

Deep in stillness, secrets wait,
Frozen memories twist and twine,
The cold weaves tales of fate,
In the silence, stars align.

Footsteps crunch on a frosty trail,
The moonlight guides, a silver veil,
Echoes linger, soft and pale,
A symphony of the night's tale.

The world seems wrapped in blue embrace,
Every moment, a frozen art,
In the dark, we find our place,
Glacial echoes stir the heart.

As dawn approaches, shadows thin,
A new light bathes the waking world,
Yet in the night, we'll always spin,
In glacial echoes, dreams unfurled.

The Graceful Fall of Snow

In gentle whispers, snow cascades,
Draping the earth in soft white shades.
Each flake a dream from winter's breath,
A silent dance of life and death.

Through barren branches, silver glows,
A quiet shroud where silence flows.
The world transforms, serene and bright,
Under the spell of purest white.

Amidst the chill, a warmth remains,
In every drift, the heart regains.
The graceful fall sings peace anew,
A lullaby from skies of blue.

As twilight falls, the shadows creep,
Yet in this stillness, secrets keep.
The gentle hush, a sweet retreat,
Where earth and heaven softly meet.

With every flake, the world is bare,
Yet beauty lingers in the air.
The winter's grace, a fleeting show,
In the embrace of falling snow.

Dreams of Crystal Stillness

In whispers soft, the night unfolds,
With crystal dreams, the heart beholds.
A world at rest, in silken sighs,
Where time stands still beneath the skies.

Each star a gem, each breath a song,
In silent realms where dreams belong.
The moonlight glimmers on the stream,
In silver waves, we drift and dream.

Voices hushed, the night is kind,
Within the calm, our souls unwind.
A tapestry of quiet grace,
In stillness found, our sacred space.

The frost defines the edges clear,
Of every thought, and every fear.
In gentle landscapes, soft and bright,
We wander through this starry night.

Each moment crystalline and true,
A dance of shadows, light breaks through.
In dreams of stillness, hearts entwine,
Together in this space divine.

The Dance of Frost and Silence

Upon the ground, the frost will weave,
A shimmering cloak, with magic cleaves.
In quiet steps, the cold winds play,
In nature's dance, both night and day.

The branches bow with snowy crowns,
In silence deep, where beauty drowns.
Each quiet moment wrapped in grace,
As whispers swell in this soft space.

A breath of chill, the air is thin,
Yet warmth ignites the soul within.
With every swirl, the crystals twirl,
A winter's waltz in a frozen whirl.

Through fields aglow in twilight's hue,
The dance continues, old yet new.
Embracing stillness, hearts take flight,
In frost and silence, pure delight.

As dawn arrives, the colors blend,
The frosty spell begins to mend.
Yet memories linger, crystal bright,
Of nights spent dancing, in the light.

Twilight's Cold Embrace

As twilight paints the sky in blue,
The world is draped in silver hue.
Each shadow stretches, reaching wide,
In cold embrace, the day must hide.

Beneath the dusk, the whispers grow,
A tender hush where feelings flow.
The stars awake, their light so pale,
As night descends, we start to sail.

In every breath, the chill resides,
A gentle pull, like swirling tides.
Through whispered winds, the secrets creep,
In twilight's arms, our dreams we keep.

A frigid kiss upon the face,
Yet in this chill, we find our place.
With hearts aglow, we seek the night,
In twilight's dance, we find the light.

So let us wander, hand in hand,
Through twilight's realm, a promised land.
In every sigh, the cold we face,
Holds beauty in twilight's cold embrace.

Tales from the Ice

Whispers travel on frozen winds,
Ancient stories the stillness rescinds.
Footprints etched in the glistening snow,
Silent witnesses to the tales that flow.

Branches hang dressed in white lace,
Nature's breath slows its frantic pace.
A flicker of light breaks through the grey,
Inviting hearts to pause and stay.

Echoes of laughter in frosted air,
Memories linger, everywhere.
Time holds its breath in this icy domain,
Each moment captured, yet never in vain.

A skater glides with effortless grace,
Traces of joy on a cold, bright face.
Underneath stars that shimmer like glass,
Night wraps around us as shadows pass.

In solitude, peace finds a hold,
Wrapped in blankets of white and gold.
With each breath, the magic ignites,
In these tales, the heart unites.

The Quiet of Chilling Nights

When the moon hangs low and the world lies still,
A hush envelops the evening chill.
Stars twinkle softly, a radiant sight,
Guiding us through the embracing night.

Frosted branches sway in the breeze,
Nature's quiet whispers echo with ease.
The crunch of snow beneath each footfall,
In this serene moment, we feel it all.

Embers glow from a distant hearth,
Warming spirits, igniting mirth.
Laughter dances on the frosty air,
A gentle reminder that love is rare.

In the stillness, dreams take flight,
Wrapped in the cloak of gentle night.
Softly, we drift on the edge of dreams,
In the quiet, nothing is as it seems.

The dark hosts secrets, wrapped in delight,
Hidden treasures sleep through the night.
Each heartbeat echoes in this sacred space,
In chilling nights, we find our place.

Silent Icy Cradle

Nurtured by the hush of the winter's breath,
Lies a world untouched by time and death.
Snowdrifts cradle the dreams we keep,
In this quiet realm, our thoughts run deep.

Beneath the stars, the silence sings,
Each breath a promise that nature brings.
Gentle snowflakes kiss the earth below,
In this icy cradle, hearts start to glow.

Clouds drift by in a fleeting trance,
While the world outside takes a second glance.
Awakened spirits in a frozen embrace,
Finding solace in this tranquil space.

Memories of laughter woven in white,
Echo softly through the stillness of night.
A frozen river murmurs its tale,
As dreams unfold in the moon's soft veil.

Time slows down in this gentle night,
Wrapped in warm whispers, pure delight.
Lulled by the charm of the snowy scene,
In this cradle of stillness, we are serene.

Frosted Memories

In the heart of winter, where shadows play,
Lies a canvas of frost, both bright and grey.
Each flake a whisper of love once known,
In the silence, memories are gently sown.

The chill brings echoes of laughter and cheer,
Moments returned, so vividly clear.
In the quiet, time bends and sways,
Frosted reflections of countless days.

Footprints linger on paths long walked,
Stories shared in warmth, softly talked.
Under the branches, the past comes alive,
In the embrace of frost, we truly thrive.

A flicker of warmth in the wintry air,
Guiding us through the cold, with care.
The fire crackles, a soft serenade,
Frosted memories, a joyful cascade.

In hidden corners of the heart's domain,
Lies a treasure of joy, love, and pain.
As winter whispers its frozen song,
In every memory, we forever belong.

Song of the Shivering Breeze

Whispers through the frozen trees,
A breath of cold, a gentle tease.
Leaves tremble, dance, and sway,
In the crisp light of the day.

Echoes of a winter's sigh,
Wrap the world, as time slips by.
Frosted fingers brush my face,
Nature's chill, a soft embrace.

Moonlit nights that sing so clear,
From the shadows, they appear.
Dreams of warmth in pale moonlight,
In the cold, our hearts ignite.

Snowflakes twirl in playful chase,
Twinkling stars in frosty lace.
Each flake tells a story true,
Of winter's love for me and you.

Breathe the air, so icy sweet,
Frosty kisses, winter's greet.
In this cold, our souls take flight,
With every shiver, hearts unite.

Frosted Hearts' Soliloquy

In the stillness, whispers form,
Frozen tales, the heart's warm storm.
Every beat a gentle snow,
Wrapped in silence, love will grow.

Chilled by doubt and warmed by hope,
Through the dark, we learn to cope.
Frosted petals, dreams that bloom,
In the cold, dispelling gloom.

Winter's breath, a soft caress,
In its grasp, we find our zest.
Hearts entwined beneath the frost,
In this dance, we'll not get lost.

Every moment glistens bright,
In the dark, we find our light.
Frosted whispers, sweet and low,
In their midst, our feelings grow.

With each sigh, the chill recedes,
In the winter, love proceeds.
Together through the snowy nights,
Frosted hearts, we soar to heights.

The Icy Murmuration

Voices blend in chilly air,
Flocks of dreams, we rise and share.
Birds in flight, a swirling dance,
In the cold, we take a chance.

Agile twists and turns they make,
A shimmering path, the frost will break.
Nature's art, a fleeting show,
Through the white, our spirits flow.

Beneath the sky, so vast and deep,
Where silent thoughts begin to creep.
Wings of hope against the chill,
Daring hearts, they fly at will.

In the frosted dusk, we converge,
On icy currents, we emerge.
A tapestry that weaves our fates,
In every beat, the magic waits.

From the shadows, futures bloom,
In the cold, we chase the gloom.
Through the night, our stories blend,
In icy murmurs, hearts transcend.

Lullabies Beneath the Frozen Surface

Gentle hymns the silence sings,
Winter's hush, a soft embrace clings.
Beneath the ice, where dreams reside,
Lullabies in whispers glide.

Every ripple tells a tale,
Of hidden worlds where spirits sail.
Crystals shimmering, secrets kept,
In the stillness, hearts have slept.

Moonlit hours, so peaceful, bright,
In the dark, we dance with light.
Songs of frost, a tender sound,
In icy depths, our love is found.

Echoes call in hush of night,
Guiding paths to warmth and light.
Through the frozen earth we roam,
In the cold, we find our home.

With every lullaby, we learn,
In winter's hold, our hearts will burn.
Beneath the frost, hopes rise anew,
In frozen dreams, I sing for you.

The Stillness in Frost

In winter's hush, the world stands still,
A blanket white, on every hill.
The breath of ice, a tranquil sigh,
As nature sleeps under the sky.

Beneath the boughs, the silence grows,
A canvas pure where stillness flows.
Each flake a whisper, soft and light,
A moment frozen, pure delight.

The trees wear coats of shimmering glaze,
Bright diamonds catch the sun's warm rays.
Footprints fade on the silver ground,
In stillness profound, peace is found.

The air is crisp, a fleeting chill,
But warmth resides in winter's thrill.
With every breath, a story told,
In frosted dreams and heartbeats bold.

So let us wander through this scene,
Where calmness reigns, and thoughts are keen.
In stillness, find the beauty's crest,
Embrace the frost, and be at rest.

Beneath the Veil of Snow

Beneath the veil of gentle snow,
The world transforms, a wondrous show.
Each flake descends like tender grace,
A soft embrace, a quiet space.

The rooftops wear a frosty crown,
As streets become a glistening gown.
In every corner, magic glows,
As winter's spell intricately shows.

The distant trees, now dressed in white,
Whisper the secrets of the night.
With every step, the crunch resounds,
In soft serenity, joy abounds.

The sky is draped in muted light,
While shadows dance in soft twilight.
A secret haven, calm and slow,
In silence deep, beneath the snow.

So let us linger in this dream,
Where silence reigns and voices gleam.
With hearts alight, we'll journey far,
Beneath the veil, where wonders are.

Glacial Murmurs

In icy realms, where whispers flow,
The glacial murmurs softly grow.
Each breath a tale of ancient ice,
As nature's voice reflects its slice.

Frozen rivers carve the land,
In silent strokes, in nature's hand.
The echoes sing of time untold,
In chilling depths, the stories hold.

Silvery shards catch fleeting light,
Bringing forth the day from night.
With each small sound, the world awakes,
In frozen beauty, the silence breaks.

Cracks and creaks, a symphony,
A melody of what will be.
In glacial arms, the stillness stirs,
Embraced by nature, calm endures.

So lend your ear to drifting sounds,
Where peace is found, and magic abounds.
In glacial murmurs, hearts align,
In winter's song, so pure, divine.

Subtle Frostbite

In shadows cast by fading light,
The subtle frostbite claims the night.
A tingle dances on the skin,
As winter's chill draws softly in.

Glistening trails where footsteps fade,
In crisp air, memories are laid.
A fleeting touch, a gentle bite,
As stars emerge in dawning light.

The breath of frost, a tender kiss,
In moments brief, we find our bliss.
Through whispered winds, the night unfolds,
A secret warmth, as winter molds.

With every breath, the cold is near,
Yet in its grasp, there's naught to fear.
For in this chill, life holds its grace,
With subtle frostbite's soft embrace.

So welcome winter's sweet caress,
In freeze and thaw, find happiness.
In each cold breath, our spirits rise,
Embraced by frost beneath the skies.

Secrets Caught in the Snow

Whispers curl in frosty air,
Footprints trace a hidden lair.
Glistening secrets, soft and bright,
Nature's canvas, purest white.

Silent tales the snowflakes weave,
In their dance, we dare believe.
Underneath their fragile grace,
Lies a world we dare not face.

Frozen echoes, soft and deep,
In their stillness, shadows creep.
Every flake a story told,
In the chill, our dreams unfold.

Bright stars twinkle in the night,
Illuminating snowy sight.
The moon, a witness to it all,
Hears the secrets as they call.

As dawn breaks, hues start to blend,
Snowy whispers find their end.
But in the heart, they still remain,
Secrets caught in winter's reign.

Last Words of Winter

The breath of frost begins to wane,
As sunbeams pierce the icy chain.
Whispers of warmth start to rise,
Winter bids its soft goodbyes.

Snowflakes drift in final flight,
Crystals shimmer in the light.
In the hush of fading chill,
Nature's pulse begins to thrill.

A blanket thick gives way to ground,
Quietly, life stirs all around.
With each thaw, the world awakes,
In the stillness, silence shakes.

Trees stretch tall, shedding white,
Painted branches, a hopeful sight.
Winter's whispers softly fade,
In the warmth, new dreams are laid.

With every ray that breaks the night,
Spring draws near with gentle light.
Last words linger, sweet and clear,
Winter's end is drawing near.

Hints of a Frozen Dream

In shadows where the silence sleeps,
Frozen dreams in stillness creep.
Icy breaths on midnight air,
Whispers brush the world with care.

Glistening secrets tucked in frost,
In the stillness, nothing lost.
Echoes of a slumber song,
In this chill, we all belong.

A fleeting glimpse of what could be,
Beneath the cold, a mystery.
Time slows down in crystal frames,
Memories wrapped in winter's claims.

With every glimmer, shadows play,
Hints of dreams that drift away.
Winter's breath within us stirs,
In frozen thoughts, our hope occurs.

As seasons shift, so do we change,
Dancing in a realm so strange.
Yet in this frost, we find our grace,
Hints of dreams in winter's embrace.

Murmurs Beneath the Ice

Underneath the surface veiled,
Murmurs of the past, unveiled.
In the depths, the whispers flow,
Tales of warmth that we don't know.

Ripples echo through the cold,
Stories waiting to be told.
In the silence, truths reside,
Beneath the ice, where dreams abide.

Frosty layers hide the light,
Cradling secrets in the night.
Every shimmer, every gleam,
Holds a piece of yesterday's dream.

As the thaw begins to call,
Murmurs rise, and echoes fall.
Nature's chorus, soft but clear,
Carries whispers, drawing near.

In the spring, they will return,
With a fire, a passion, a burn.
Yet here they linger, calm and nice,
Sweet murmurs trapped beneath the ice.

Frosted Secrets

In the silence, whispers lie,
Frozen secrets in the sky.
Snowflakes falling, soft and white,
Hiding truths from the light.

Footprints trace a hidden tale,
Beneath the frost, dreams prevail.
Nature's breath, a quiet sigh,
In the stillness, spirits fly.

Shadows dance on icy streams,
Echoing the heart's lost dreams.
Winter's veil, a tender shroud,
Silent stories, fierce and proud.

Echoes of a Frozen Heart

In chambers cold, echoes swell,
Frozen heart, a silent spell.
Where warmth once bloomed, now lies freeze,
Memories drift upon the breeze.

Each crack a sigh, a whispered plea,
Longing for what used to be.
Shattered dreams and silent tears,
Time stands still as hope clears.

Echoes haunt the empty halls,
Through icy barriers, sorrow calls.
In shadows deep, where darkness lingers,
Lies the warmth of fleeting fingers.

Spheres of Lament

Round the fire, shadows play,
Spheres of lament drift away.
Each flicker a story, tales untold,
Of love and loss, both fierce and bold.

Dancing flames, a bittersweet glow,
Whispering secrets we used to know.
The weight of silence fills the night,
In every spark, a wish for flight.

Time spins slowly, dreams entwined,
Echoes of a broken mind.
In circles drawn, the past takes flight,
Spheres of lament in the fading light.

Shivering Melodies

In the twilight, notes arise,
Shivering melodies fill the skies.
A soft refrain, a distant call,
Whispers weaving through the fall.

Frosted winds like gentle hands,
Playing songs by winter's bands.
Each tone, a memory's embrace,
In icy realms, we find our place.

Notes entwined in moonlight's seam,
Dance like shadows, blend like dream.
In shivers sweet, the night bestows,
Melodies where the heart still flows.

Fragments of Frosted Dreams

In whispers caught on winter's breath,
Visions glint like shards of glass.
Silent tales of dreams long spent,
Echoing where shadows pass.

Moonlight drapes the world in ice,
A silver shroud on slumbered ground.
Each glimmer holds a hidden price,
Where memories and chill are found.

Frosted petals softly fall,
Blanketing the silent trees.
Each flake a story, faint and small,
Weaving through the evening breeze.

Time drips slow like melting snow,
Across the vast and endless night.
Frozen sighs begin to grow,
A symphony of pure delight.

In the stillness, dreams take flight,
With every spark of icy gleam.
Fragments dance in soft moonlight,
A tapestry of whispered dreams.

The Softest Chill

Through hushed whispers, winds do tell,
Of magic wrapped in frosted air.
The softest chill, a wondrous spell,
Embracing hearts without a care.

Stars twinkle like frozen tears,
Glimmers of hope in the night sky.
Beneath the cloak of winter's peers,
The world breathes deep, a muted sigh.

A blanket thick, both pure and white,
Covers each branch with tender grace.
In stillness found, the world feels right,
Embracing peace in this cold place.

The sound of silence, crisp and clear,
Cocooning dreams in velvet threads.
The softness draws the heart near,
As winter whispers where it treads.

In every flake, a wish ignites,
A promise made with gentle hands.
The chill that wraps the longest nights,
Becomes the warmth of winter's bands.

Symphony of the Frost

A symphony of frost and air,
Composed in notes of winter's chill.
Beneath the boughs, a world laid bare,
As twilight falls, the dreams fulfill.

Each crystal flake a tiny chime,
Dances soft beneath the moon.
In harmony, they mark the time,
Their rhythm sings a frosty tune.

The trees conduct with graceful sway,
As icy whispers weave their sound.
Nature's song in soft decay,
A serenade to winter found.

Amidst the cold, a warmth ignites,
Within the heart, a gentle glow.
The symphony of day and nights,
Unfolds in beauty, pure and slow.

With every breath, a new refrain,
A melody of quiet grace.
In winter's hold, we feel no pain,
For harmony in cold we trace.

Hidden Sagas of the Cold World

Beneath the frost, tales lie in wait,
In blankets thick of whispered snow.
Hidden sagas, sealed by fate,
In every flake, the stories flow.

Roots interlaced beneath the ground,
Keep secrets shared through time's embrace.
In silence found, a truth is drowned,
Yet lingers on in nature's grace.

Frozen rivers, still as night,
Guard the echoes of ages past.
In their depths, the hidden light,
Reflects the world in shadows cast.

Footsteps crunch on pathways white,
Each echo tells of journeys made.
As whispers dance in soft twilight,
The cold unveils what time portrayed.

In every gust, a story swirls,
A tapestry of warm regret.
The cold world spins with quiet pearls,
Of hidden sagas we forget.

Shards of Silence

In stillness lies a fragile sound,
Echoes trapped, no voice is found.
The whispers weave through shadowed night,
A tapestry of lost delight.

A breath of air, a fleeting thought,
In moments caught, the silence sought.
Time stands still, a gentle sigh,
In shards of peace, the heart will fly.

The world outside begins to fade,
In this cocoon, desires are laid.
Threads of hope, a quiet plea,
Caught between what is and be.

Nature hushes, all is calm,
A soothing balm, a silent psalm.
In the void, the soul will dance,
Embracing shadows, taking chance.

So linger here, where echoes blend,
In shattered peace, our hearts will mend.
In shards of silence, we find grace,
A sacred space, a warm embrace.

The Dance of Winter's Breath

Snowflakes whisper upon the ground,
Each one a story, softly crowned.
As winter breathes, the world turns white,
A frozen canvas, pure delight.

Branches sway under silver skies,
In the stillness, magic lies.
Frosted leaves, a glimmering show,
Nature's dance in shimmering glow.

Footprints trace where lovers tread,
In this chill, warm words are said.
The hearth ignites, the shadows play,
Each flicker calls the night to stay.

The world in slumber, wrapped so tight,
Awaits the promise of dawn's light.
In winter's arms, all is serene,
A moment held, a tranquil dream.

So let us twirl in this embrace,
In winter's breath, find our place.
Together, hearts in rhythm beat,
In the dance of cold, our souls meet.

Secrets in the Frost

Beneath the surface, secrets hide,
In glistening frost, they bide their time.
Each crystal formed, a tale retold,
In whispers soft, their truths unfold.

Patterns etched in icy lace,
Nature's art, a fleeting grace.
With every chill, memories surface,
In frozen whispers, lives may converse.

Underneath the frost, hearts learn,
Of lost loves and the fires that burn.
Cold winds carry shadows deep,
While the world wraps in quiet sleep.

Secrets linger, they yearn to speak,
In silence vast, the moments peek.
Embrace the cold, allow it in,
For within the frost, new dreams begin.

Let us wander through this maze,
Find warmth inside winter's gaze.
Secrets in the frost unite,
In the hush of cold, we find the light.

Crystal Lullabies

Stars adorn the velvet night,
In the stillness, soft and bright.
Whispers float on gentle wings,
The nightingale, it sweetly sings.

Crystals glisten, dreams take flight,
Wrapped in silver, purest light.
A lullaby from realms unknown,
In crystal hearts, love has grown.

The moon bestows her tender grace,
Kissing shadows, time will race.
In every note, a story glows,
Of nights embraced and laughter flows.

Feel the magic, close your eyes,
In this moment, shadows rise.
The world outside may fade away,
In crystal lullabies, we'll sway.

As dawn approaches, softly hum,
These lullabies, forever come.
In dreams we weave, forever stay,
In crystal lullabies, we'll play.

Wisdom of the Winter Wind

The winter wind whispers low,
Carrying tales of the snow.
Each flake a story untold,
In the chill, wisdom unfolds.

It dances through the barren trees,
Rustling leaves that once had ease.
In its breath, there's a knowing,
Of cycles ending and then glowing.

Listen well to its gentle sighs,
Underneath the vast gray skies.
For nature speaks in its own way,
In winter's grasp, we learn to stay.

The frost is sharp but teaches clear,
Of patience held within the sphere.
Every gust a guide to behold,
In its embrace, the heart is bold.

So when the chill begins to bite,
Find solace in the quiet night.
For wisdom finds its strength, you see,
In the winter wind, wild and free.

Frost-Fingered Charms

Frost fingers dance on windowpanes,
Each touch, a beauty, each breath, gains.
Nature's artistry, a fleeting show,
In chilly marbles, dreams do glow.

Winding paths of icy lace,
Trace the beauty with silent grace.
Crystals twinkle in morning light,
A magic spell, soft and bright.

Each corner holds a charm profound,
In every glimmer, love is found.
The world adorned in silvery hue,
Whispers of wonders waiting for you.

In this realm of frozen delight,
All worries fade as day meets night.
Breathe in the stillness, pure and clear,
Frost-fingered charms bring warmth near.

So lift your eyes to the sky above,
Frost dances lightly, shaped by love.
Hold onto the magic, ever so rare,
In winter's embrace, feel the care.

Icebound Emotion

Beneath the ice, emotions freeze,
A heart encased, longing to please.
Whispers echo, trapped in time,
A silent rhythm, a muted chime.

Frozen tears on a silent cheek,
Words unsaid leave the heart weak.
In chill embraces, dreams are lost,
Yet warmth remains at any cost.

Time moves slowly, a fragile thread,
Awakening warmth, where hope is spread.
Shattered barriers, thaw the soul,
In the depths lies the hidden whole.

Icicles hang like silent fears,
Stalactites forming from held-back tears.
But as the sun begins to rise,
Icebound emotion starts to prize.

Each drop of warmth can melt the cold,
Releasing tales that once were told.
With every thaw, the heart takes flight,
Breaking free to embrace the light.

Whispers in a Frigid Dawn

The dawn breaks crisp, a muted hue,
Whispers flutter in sky so blue.
Frozen breath of a new day found,
As nature stirs, with a gentle sound.

Softly glistening, the world awakes,
Each step, a crunch that softly breaks.
In the stillness, the heart beats slow,
Cradled in winter's gentle glow.

Whispers dance on the icy breeze,
Carrying secrets through barren trees.
Promises linger in frosty air,
In every moment, a tender care.

As sunlight spills, the shadows play,
Painting dreams along the way.
Hope ignites in the chill so bold,
In whispers of warmth, life is told.

So heed the dawn, in its frigid breath,
Embrace the stillness, conquer the death.
For in the whispers of morning's glow,
Lies the beauty of all we know.

Murmurs Beneath the Glaze

Whispers float on icy air,
Silent tales of what once was.
Beneath the frost, the secrets swell,
Memories wrap in shimmering cause.

Glimmers dance on frozen streams,
Echoes of a past alive.
Nature's hush, a subtle tease,
In the stillness, dreams survive.

Crisp leaves crackle underfoot,
Each step stirs the silent night.
Glazed branches hold breathless thoughts,
Where shadows play in pale moonlight.

The world asleep, a tranquil sigh,
Beneath the glaze, the heartbeats thrum.
In winter's clasp, we find our way,
Through whispered winds, we softly come.

Murmurs rise where cold winds play,
Cradled by the silver trees.
In every flake, a story waits,
Beneath the glaze, our spirits freeze.

Crystalline Dreams

In the dawn, the light unfolds,
Casting shards of bright allure.
Every glimmer, a wish retold,
In crystalline dreams, we find our cure.

Snowflakes drift like gentle sighs,
Embroidering the world in white.
Softly placed like lullabies,
Each spark a stroke of pure delight.

Daylight breaks, the silence glows,
Nature's canvas, dazzling bright.
In the stillness, the magic flows,
We dance in dreams on winter's night.

Every breath a shimmering hue,
Caught within the frozen air.
We chase the light, the visions due,
In crystalline dreams, our hearts lay bare.

Ethereal beauty, a fleeting thrill,
Moments captured, time stands still.
In this world, our wishes gleam,
Lost in the quiet of crystalline dreams.

The Quiet of Frozen Days

Stillness blankets the weary land,
Each breath an echo, soft and low.
Nature holds its frozen hand,
Laying peace in shimmering snow.

Gray skies weave a gentle shroud,
Hushed whispers in the chilling air.
In silence, dreams are avowed,
A world reborn, so strangely rare.

Frosted panes frame quiet views,
The world wrapped in a crystal cloak.
In every flake, the spirit cues,
A rhythm soft, a hidden stroke.

With every step, the whispers grow,
Footprints nestle in the frost.
In the quiet, we come to know,
What beauty lies in moments lost.

The frozen days embrace the hearts,
Cocooned in winter's gentle hold.
In silent peace, the longing starts,
The quiet of frozen days unfolds.

Secrets in a Shattered Breeze

A breeze whispers through the trees,
Its secrets dancing on the air.
In the rustling leaves, we tease,
Mysteries wrapped in nature's care.

Every gust, a fleeting touch,
Revealing tales both old and new.
Sunlight weaves with shadows such,
In the dance, we find what's true.

Clouds break open, a gentle sigh,
Breezes carry harmonies sweet.
In the hush, the spirits fly,
Where earth and sky in stillness meet.

Secrets swirled in zephyrs light,
Awaken dreams in every heart.
In whispers soft, the world feels right,
Every breath a work of art.

A shattered breeze, a tender song,
In its flow, our hopes entwine.
We linger where the moments throng,
Secrets found in breezes fine.

Hushed Crystals

In the silence, whispers flow,
Crystals shimmer, soft and low.
Moonlight dances on the frost,
In this beauty, we are lost.

Glistening gems upon the ground,
Frozen treasures all around.
Nature's art, a fleeting sight,
Wrapped in magic, pure delight.

Quiet sighs of chilly air,
Echo softly everywhere.
Each breath floats like silver dreams,
Awakening the night's quiet themes.

In stillness, memories reside,
Underneath the icy tide.
Each moment holds a world anew,
Hushed and crystal, bright and true.

Tales from the Frozen Abyss

Deep beneath the chilling waves,
Lies the realm where darkness saves.
Whales sing songs of ages past,
In this silence, echoes last.

Frosted currents, ancient lore,
Skeletons of ships explore.
Whispers of the lost at sea,
Guarded by serenity.

Shadows flicker in the depths,
Zooplankton dance, their quiet steps.
Time is still, yet ever flows,
In the abyss where no one goes.

Icebergs tower, massive and grand,
Holding secrets of the land.
Stories etched in icy tears,
Carved by nature, lost for years.

Each wave tells a tale untold,
In the dark, where dreams unfold.
Frozen truths, a silent kiss,
Whispers deep from the abyss.

Icy Reveries

Draped in silver, morning breaks,
Twinkling on the frozen lakes.
A dance of light in gentle sway,
Icy dreams greet the day.

Clouds hang low, a misty veil,
Frosted echoes, soft and pale.
Chilled whispers soothe the waking earth,
In this moment, find your worth.

Footsteps crunch in purest white,
Through the calm of frosted night.
Each breath we take, a crystal sigh,
In this realm where spirits fly.

Nature's hymn, a soft refrain,
Blankets wrapped in winter's gain.
In reflection, stillness found,
Icy reveries swirl around.

As night descends, the stars ignite,
Painted gems in the velvet night.
Dreams take flight on silver wings,
In the chill, a warmth that sings.

Frostbitten Lullabies

Whispers drift on winter's breath,
Softly cradling dreams from death.
Frostbitten lullabies entwine,
Holding close, the heart's design.

Snowflakes drift like whispers down,
Wrapping peace in a gentle gown.
Nature sings a soothing tune,
Underneath the slumbering moon.

In the quiet, shadows blend,
Every heartbeat finds its end.
Cold embraces, tender grace,
In this frozen, sacred space.

Gentle streams of icy flow,
Carry tales from long ago.
Echoes hum a lullaby,
As stars twinkle in the sky.

When dawn breaks with hues so bright,
Frosty dreams take flight in light.
In the morning, warmth shall greet,
The frosted lullabies retreat.

Frozen Echoes

In twilight's grip, whispers roam,
Echoes entwined, far from home.
Crystal shards in the moon's light,
Frozen dreams take flight tonight.

Softly they call, the past so near,
A symphony strung on frozen fear.
Each note a tear from distant time,
Resonating in a hushed chime.

Snowflakes dance on a stillened air,
Memories linger, a solemn prayer.
The world asleep beneath the frost,
In silence, all that we've lost.

Sparkling whispers in the night,
As shadows flicker, dim and slight.
Through branches bare, light's remnants play,
In frozen echoes, night turns to day.

Yet amidst the chill, warmth can bloom,
In heart's embrace, dispelling gloom.
For even in winter's tightest squeeze,
Hope stirs gently, a breath, a tease.

Shards of Silence

In the void where shadows fade,
Silence forms a fragile blade.
Cutting through the silent night,
Shattered dreams in pale moonlight.

Each glimmer hides a tale untold,
Of warm hearts turned to bitter cold.
Shards of silence, sharp and clear,
Echoes caught in frozen air.

Between the breaths, a moment stays,
A thousand thoughts, a silent maze.
Wandering through the chilling dark,
Searching for a fleeting spark.

Time stands still in the frozen beam,
Reality trapped in a hazy dream.
Voices lost in a spectral haze,
Shards of silence in the winter's blaze.

Frost-covered whispers, soft and light,
Drifting gently into the night.
In the stillness, we find our way,
Through shards of silence, come what may.

Beneath the Frosted Breath

Beneath the frost, a world lies still,
Softly waiting, fit to fill.
Silent secrets, buried deep,
In frozen drifts, where shadows creep.

The breath of winter holds its gaze,
On icy paths, a tender maze.
Where every glimmer hides a trace,
Of fleeting warmth, a soft embrace.

Stars above flicker and shine,
Illuminating the frozen line.
In the hush, a heart can yearn,
For the fire's glow, the warm return.

Beneath the frost, life's pulse remains,
In whispered hopes, in silent chains.
The world spins on, though cold and bare,
Dreaming of spring in the frosted air.

Yet, in the stillness, time can heal,
As hope awaits beneath the wheel.
With each thaw, life dares to ignite,
Beneath the frost, the spark is bright.

Secrets in Glacial Shadows

In glacial shadows, secrets sleep,
In whispered winds, their silence deep.
The frost conceals what hearts once knew,
Darkened tales in a crystal hue.

Beneath the ice, a story weaves,
Of love, of loss, in tangled leaves.
Flickering light reveals the past,
In shadows thick, truth holds steadfast.

Winds of change brush against the night,
While snowflakes whisper, soft and light.
Stories echo through the frigid air,
In glacial shadows, no one is there.

Frosted illusions dance and sway,
As twilight slips into the gray.
Each secret held beneath the freeze,
Yearns for the sun, the gentle breeze.

Yet under layers, life will stir,
In icy depths, hearts still confer.
For even shadows can reveal,
The warmth found in the cold, surreal.

Lattice of Shivers

In the quiet night, shadows play,
Whispering secrets in shades of gray.
A chill in the air, a soft, sharp breath,
Threads of frost weave tales of death.

Pale moonlight dances on the ground,
Casting dreams where lost hopes are found.
Each tremor spreads like ripples wide,
Painting the world where fears abide.

Branches tremble in the icy breeze,
Nature's heartbeat slows with ease.
A lattice formed from winter's hand,
Bound by silence, a ghostly band.

Echoes linger in the dark,
Murmurs lost, a fading spark.
In the cold embrace of this night,
The shivers weave a tapestry tight.

Glasses of ice on windows gleam,
Fractured light, a broken dream.
Frigid wishes float and fade,
In the lattice where fears invade.

Glacial Reflections

In the mirror of the lake, ice sleeps,
Secrets hidden, the silence keeps.
Mountains rise like ancient kings,
Guardians of dreams that winter brings.

Crystals form with a breath divine,
A shimmering world where shadows twine.
Each ripple stirs the frozen past,
Echoes linger, shadows cast.

Light fractures through the icy shield,
Revealing truths the frost concealed.
A haunting beauty, stark and clear,
In glacial depths, all is sincere.

Time stands still in this frozen grove,
Memories fade, yet never rove.
Each reflection, a story spun,
In delicate threads, together as one.

Underneath like whispers lie,
The dreams we lost, the reasons why.
In stillness, the heart learns to see,
The glacial whispers that set us free.

The Still Heart of Winter

In the forest deep, silence reigns,
Winter's breath, a gentle chain.
The world, wrapped in a frosty shroud,
Listening close, immersed in crowd.

Branches bow with a frozen grace,
Time flows slow, a solemn pace.
Each flake that falls, a whispered prayer,
Entranced beneath the silver glare.

Beneath the stillness, life beats on,
In frozen hearts, dawn's light has shone.
Though the night lingers, hope remains,
In the cold embrace of winter's chains.

Stars pinned tight in the velvet sky,
Guarding dreams that dare to fly.
Wrapped in stillness, the heart will find,
A warmth that lies within the mind.

So let the cold kiss your skin,
For in the heart, the dream begins.
The stillness holds what time won't take,
In the depth of winter, the spirit wakes.

Echoes Trapped in Crystal

In icy halls where whispers tread,
Echoes of laughter, long since dead.
Captured in crystal, moments freeze,
Time's gentle hand brought to its knees.

Beneath the frost, the memories hum,
A symphony of where we've come.
Each note, a story, soft yet clear,
Rippling softly, bringing near.

Frozen rifts where shadows flow,
Trapped in the silence, dreams gallop slow.
Every flicker, a tale to tell,
In the heart of winter, bound in shell.

The glassy surface reflects the past,
While moments linger, shadows cast.
In splintered light, echoes will rise,
A chorus born from starlit skies.

Entwined in stories, they waltz and sway,
In the stillness of a winter's day.
Through each crystal, a life defined,
Echoes whispering what's left behind.

Murmurs of the Arctic Night

Stars shimmer bright in the sky,
While the northern winds softly sigh.
Whispers of ice in the moon's glow,
Secrets of ages long ago.

Shadows dance on the frost-kissed ground,
Echoes of silence, a haunting sound.
In the stillness, the world does pause,
Nature's beauty, forever draws.

New horizons break with dawn's light,
Painting the canvas, pure and white.
Footprints fade where the wild things roam,
In this frozen, timeless home.

Tales of the aurora's embrace,
Glimmers of hope in a cold place.
Murmurs weave through the endless night,
Dreams take flight on wings of light.

The Arctic's heart beats strong and true,
Clad in a mantle of brilliant blue.
Each breath a story, each moment rare,
In the chill of night, the world lays bare.

Silent Winter's Whisper

Snowflakes drift in the gentle breeze,
Whispers softly through the frozen trees.
A tranquil hush blankets the ground,
In this stillness, peace is found.

Frosty patterns on the windowpane,
Nature's artwork born of cold rain.
Silhouettes glide in the pale moonlight,
As time stands still on this winter's night.

Stars twinkle like diamonds on high,
Bathed in the glow of a velvet sky.
Each breath released forms a cloud,
In solitude, silence is proud.

Beneath the surface, life still stirs,
Whispers of warmth in the heart occurs.
Winter's embrace, both harsh and sweet,
In its stillness, all souls meet.

Silent echoes of the night,
Cradled within a blanket of white.
Awakening springs from this frozen peace,
In each quiet moment, time may cease.

Frosted Footprints

In the snow where whispers dwell,
Footprints tell a story, a spell.
Each step speaks of journeys long,
In crisp air, where echoes belong.

Frosted trails lead to the unknown,
Pathways marked where the wild have flown.
Curious creatures dance and play,
Tracing memories of the day.

Sunrise spills gold on a silver field,
Promises of warmth as winter yields.
Footprints fade with the warming light,
Yet their imprint lingers in the night.

Amidst the trees, shadows intertwine,
Storytellers of a realm divine.
Every crunch beneath the boots,
Whispers of life, where adventure roots.

Frosted footsteps lead us through,
Navigating paths born anew.
In every turn, a tale unfolds,
Nature's secrets waiting to be told.

Chronicles of Winter's Breath

Chill winds carry a tale untold,
Of winter's magic, quiet and bold.
Fires dance with warmth in the air,
While dreams take flight, free from care.

The world is a canvas, painted white,
Silhouettes in the fading light.
Branches creak under crystal weight,
Nature's beauty, a silent mate.

Icicles hang like glass from eaves,
Glistening jewels amongst the leaves.
Footsteps crunch on the frosted ground,
In every pause, life's stories abound.

Chapters fold in the winter's haze,
Fleeting moments in a snowy maze.
Breath of the season, crisp and clear,
Whispers of wonder, drawing near.

As night descends with a gentle sigh,
Constellations light the frosty sky.
Chronicles woven in shimmering threads,
In winter's breath, where magic spreads.

Secrets of the Frozen Breath

In the hush of winter's hold,
Whispers weave through drifts of cold.
Secrets speak in icy air,
Echoes linger everywhere.

Frosty tendrils dance and glide,
Beneath the moon, they softly bide.
Crystals shimmer, truths unfold,
Mysteries in silence told.

Brittle silence, sharp and clear,
Carried by the winds of fear.
Time stands still, it dares to wait,
In frozen realms, we contemplate.

Glistening breath upon the glass,
Nature's art, a fleeting pass.
Hidden stories, tightly spun,
Frozen tales of all we've done.

With each sigh, the air ignites,
Oldest secrets in the nights.
Beneath the ice, the world sleeps tight,
Waiting for the dawn's first light.

The Chill Beneath

Beneath the layers, whispers sigh,
Chilled fingers touch the still night sky.
Frost-kissed dreams in shadows creep,
The chill beneath, where secrets sleep.

Softly drift the silent flakes,
Nature's breath in frozen wakes.
Tales entwined in shivers found,
In the chill, fate's echoes sound.

Winter's cloak, a gauzy veil,
Hides the truths, both weak and frail.
In the depths, the silence swells,
A hidden realm where darkness dwells.

Branches bow with heavy frost,
Memories linger, never lost.
In the stillness, hearts may quake,
From the chill, new paths we make.

Snowflakes dance on whispered ground,
Barely uttered, hardly found.
Through the chill, we wander deep,
In the shadows, promises keep.

Frozen Whimsy

In a world of silver dreams,
Winter paints with frosted beams.
Whimsy twirls on every branch,
As if the snowflakes take a chance.

Crystalline laughter fills the air,
Tickles, teasing everywhere.
Joy in cold, a sweet delight,
Frozen whimsies spark the night.

Underneath the starlit glow,
Nature dances, soft and slow.
Each flake tells a story new,
Of frosted secrets, whispered blue.

Frosted wonders, pure and bright,
Drift like gnomes in the pale light.
In the stillness, magic flows,
As the frozen laughter grows.

Come, let's spin in winter's play,
Let our hearts lead us away.
In the chill, we'll find our glee,
Embracing joys both wild and free.

The Still Waters of Winter

Still waters, glassy, calm as night,
Reflecting stars, a tranquil sight.
Nature's breath, both soft and deep,
In winter's hush, the world does sleep.

Rippling thoughts beneath the freeze,
Memories drift like whispering trees.
Captured stillness, time stands still,
Silent moments, the heart to fill.

Frozen echoes gently sway,
Carried forth in the frosty play.
Beneath the sheen, a heartbeat glows,
In quiet depths, the silence grows.

Moonlight kisses icy streams,
Where dreams awaken from their seams.
The world holds breath, awaiting spring,
In still waters, life will sing.

Hold the peace, this fleeting hour,
In winter's grasp, we find the power.
A mirror of the heart's soft woe,
In the stillness, love we sow.

Glinting Whispers

In the heart of the night,
Stars twinkle and gleam,
Whispers of dreams take flight,
Carried by moonlit beams.

Echoes of laughter play,
Among the shadows cast,
Gentle winds sway and sway,
Treasured moments hold fast.

Silhouettes dance in light,
Painting the sky so bright,
Glimmers of hope ignite,
In the silence of night.

The world feels so alive,
Each breath a secret shared,
In this glinting archive,
Feelings laid bare, unprepared.

As dawn begins to glow,
Whispers fade into air,
Yet in the heart, we know,
Love lingers everywhere.

Frost-kissed Thoughts

A chill drapes over morn,
As frost begins to lace,
Each tree a tale reborn,
In winter's soft embrace.

Thoughts wander through the mist,
Chasing the fleeting light,
In silence, dreams persist,
Wrapped in warm hopes so bright.

Nature's canvas unfolds,
With crystals pure and clear,
Whispers of secrets told,
In the biting atmosphere.

Every breath is a cloud,
In the crisp, biting air,
Moments lost in the crowd,
Where solace meets despair.

Yet beauty holds its ground,
In the shimmering frost,
In thoughts that swirl around,
It's warmth that we have lost.

The Echoing Chill

Winter whispers in tones,
A chill that grips the soul,
With each gust, it moans,
While shadows start to roll.

Steps crunch on the ground,
A symphony of white,
In silence, peace is found,
As day surrenders night.

Echoes of laughter fade,
Into the frosty air,
Yet memories are made,
In moments we must share.

The breath of icy winds,
Carries stories untold,
In every glance, it sends,
A warmth against the cold.

As twilight paints the sky,
With hues of deepening blue,
The echoing chill sighs,
In the heart, it feels true.

Silent Pathways of Frost

Footsteps on the path,
Crunching softly below,
In nature's quiet wrath,
Where the frostflowers grow.

Glistening under light,
Each blade a tiny star,
We walk through the night,
Not knowing where we are.

Branches bear their weight,
Adorned in sparkling white,
Silent, still, they wait,
For the dawning of light.

Every breath we take,
Is a whisper of dreams,
On this journey we make,
Through the frost's gentle seams.

In the hush of the woods,
Where time seems to stand still,
The chill echoes like moods,
In the heart's quiet thrill.

Murmurs of the Winter Veil

The trees stand tall in silent grace,
As whispers drift in winter's face.
A blanket white, a crisp embrace,
Where time stands still in this cold space.

Footsteps crunch on frosty ground,
In nature's hush, a peace is found.
The world is wrapped, a soft profound,
In winter's veil, joy does abound.

The air is sharp, yet dreams unfold,
With tales of warmth, in nights so cold.
Each breath a cloud, a story told,
In frosts of silver, bright and bold.

Stars peek down from skies so deep,
In this still night, the world does sleep.
While shadows dance, the secrets keep,
In winter's heart, the magic steeps.

From each soft flake, a wonder springs,
As melodies in silence sing.
With every chill, the hope it brings,
In murmurs sweet, the season clings.

The Chilling Composition

A symphony of ice and snow,
In frigid air, the cold winds blow.
Each flake a note, in softest glow,
A chilling tune that steals the show.

The moonlight casts a silver hue,
As shadows stretch and whispers brew.
Nature's choir, a solemn crew,
In winter's grip, we're born anew.

Crystals dance on frosty breath,
In winter's grasp, there lies no death.
With every chill, we draw a depth,
A song of life, with each bequeath.

The trees adorned in white's embrace,
Where time retreats, all things find space.
In freezing winds, we feel its grace,
A chilling composition, we trace.

As dawn breaks through the icy veil,
The world awakens, life prevails.
In winter's grip, no heart can fail,
Together we sing in harmony's trail.

Echoes in the Snow

With each step made on glistening white,
The echoes whisper in the night.
A soft refrain, a pure delight,
In snowy realms, the world feels right.

The winds do carry tales untold,
Of winters past, as they unfold.
In layers thick, the stories hold,
Through frozen scenes, the dreams are bold.

As stars alight in velvet skies,
They twinkle down with ancient sighs.
The silence speaks, no need for lies,
In echoes here, the heart complies.

Each flake that falls, a note in time,
In rhythmic beats, a silent rhyme.
Through winter's song, we climb and climb,
To capture peace in simple chime.

So let us wander through the glow,
Where harmony and beauty flow.
In every step, our hopes will grow,
Amongst the whispers, echoes slow.

Serenade of the Snowflakes

A gentle waltz through winter's night,
Where snowflakes fall, a lovely sight.
Each flake unique, with pure delight,
A serenade of softest light.

The hush of cold wraps round the trees,
As frozen breaths dance with the breeze.
The world transforms, a soft reprise,
In silver dreams, our hearts find ease.

Through dusky paths of purest white,
Where shadows linger, dreams take flight.
Each twirl and spin, a pure delight,
In winter's grasp, we feel what's right.

The nightingale sings her sweetest tune,
As moonbeams weave beneath the moon.
In frosted fields, life's bright balloon,
A serenade, a soft commune.

So gather 'round, let hearts collide,
Amongst the snow, our fears subside.
In winter's calm, we shall abide,
In serenades, our souls confide.

Frozen Imprints

In the snow, footprints linger,
Memories etched on the ground.
Whispers of laughter and cheer,
Echoes in silence abound.

Icicles hang like diamonds,
Glistening under the pale moon.
Each shimmering shard a reminder,
Of warmth that comes far too soon.

Branches draped in a crystal coat,
Nature dons her frosty dress.
A world wrapped in winter's embrace,
Hiding secrets, we must confess.

Subtle Hints of Winter

A breath of chill in the air,
Hints of snow dance through the trees.
Whispers of winter's soft touch,
Carried by the very breeze.

Timid flakes begin to fall,
Kissing the earth with delight.
Each one a delicate wonder,
Bringing magic to the night.

The world slows down, whispers fade,
Wrapped in a blanket of white.
A gentle reminder of rest,
Before the spring's fiery light.

The Calm Before the Thaw

Stillness blankets the landscape,
As dusk lays its hand on the day.
The sky holds its breath to watch,
In silence, the cold winds play.

Frosty patterns lace the glass,
Nature's own quiet art.
Moments frozen in stillness,
Before spring's bold rebirth starts.

A watchful moon casts her glow,
Over fields of frozen dreams.
Preparing the world for the shift,
As hope glimmers and beams.

Frost Eternal

Frost that sparkles in the dawn,
Painting the world a brilliant hue.
Each blade of grass adorned in white,
A canvas fresh and new.

The trees stand tall, a solemn guard,
While shadows stretch long in the light.
Beneath, the earth rests, dreaming deep,
Awaiting warmth's return bright.

Moments pass in a crystalline hush,
Time dances on frozen streams.
Winter holds her breath for now,
As we linger in frosty dreams.

Veils of Cold

Whispers dance in the biting air,
Shrouded trails where silence dares.
Frosted whispers on winter's breath,
Veils of cold, a ghostly wreath.

Branches bow under heavy weight,
Silent stillness holds their fate.
In the shadows, secrets dwell,
Frozen tales they cannot tell.

The moon peers through a misty veil,
Casting shadows in a pale trail.
Every flake a story sent,
A world of whispers, cold and bent.

Footprints linger, then they fade,
Paths once warm now coldly laid.
Nature's hush, a sacred song,
In veils of cold, we all belong.

Hushed Frostfall

Gentle flakes from the sky descend,
Hushed whispers on the breeze they send.
Each flake lands with a soft embrace,
In the stillness, they find their place.

Dawn breaks slowly, a muted glow,
Painting scenes in soft white flow.
Nature's canvas, pure and bright,
Hushed frostfall, a winter's night.

Trees adorned in icy sheen,
Sparkling gems in white serene.
Footprints lead to where we wander,
In this magic, we gaze and ponder.

With every breath, the cold air bites,
Yet warmth resides in winter nights.
Underneath the sparkling crust,
Hushed frostfall, in silence, trust.

In the distance, shadows play,
Moments frozen in time's sway.
Winter's breath a calming call,
In the heart of hushed frostfall.

The Language of Snowflakes

Snowflakes whisper in the dark,
Each one holds a tiny spark.
In their fall, a tale unfolds,
The language of snowflakes, pure and bold.

A silent dance from heaven's gate,
Intricate forms that captivate.
Gone too soon, each flake divine,
Nature's art, a moment in time.

They drift and swirl in the chilly air,
Painting the world beyond compare.
On lips and lashes, soft they land,
The language of snowflakes, softly planned.

Under the moon, they're free to roam,
Each flake a traveler, seeking home.
In their journey, beauty lives,
The language of snowflakes, it gives.

Forever fleeting, never the same,
In their brief life, they play a game.
Cherished moments, we let them stay,
In the dance of winter's ballet.

Secrets Embedded in Ice

Beneath the surface, secrets hide,
In shards of glass where shadows bide.
Frozen dreams locked in a trance,
Secrets embedded, a chilling dance.

Nature's mirror reflects the past,
Whispers of time frozen fast.
Each crack a riddle, each line a clue,
In the heart of ice, stories brew.

Echoes linger in the still of night,
Hidden depths filled with ghostly light.
The icy floor, a truth untold,
Where dreams and memories unfold.

Under the surface, silence reigns,
Yet every glance, a hint remains.
In the beauty of frost, secrets find,
A fragile world, intertwined.

With every thaw, the stories gleam,
Washing over like a waking dream.
Nature's palette soft as lace,
Secrets embedded, an icy embrace.

The Stillness of a Frigid Night

The moon hangs low, a silver thread,
Whispers of frost crisp the air,
Stars blink softly in the dark,
Echoing dreams of the night rare.

Shadows stretch in silent grace,
Each breath hangs like frozen dew,
A tranquil hush, the world asleep,
Wrapped in winter's cloak, so blue.

Branches bow with a heavy weight,
Snowflakes dance in gentle flight,
Nature breathes in softest tones,
The stillness grips the heart so tight.

Footsteps fade on the snowy ground,
The warmth of home glows from afar,
In this calm, a peace is found,
Guided by the northern star.

Time stands still beneath the night,
Each moment, a breath of the cold,
In the frigid stillness we find,
The stories that the darkness holds.

Glimmering Secrets of the Cold

Icicles dangle like crystal spears,
Glistening under the waning light,
Secrets are whispered on the wind,
In the cold, the world feels right.

Patterns weave upon the snow,
Stories told by the midnight breeze,
Each flake a tale of ages past,
Captured in winter's gentle freeze.

Frost-kissed branches creak and sigh,
In their slumber, they still stand proud,
Holding dreams in icy hands,
Under the cloak of a deep white shroud.

The lake reflects a distant glow,
Echoes dance on the surface clear,
Beneath the ice, the river flows,
Keeping secrets that not all hear.

In the silence, a laughter lingers,
Tales of wonder, old and bold,
Together we listen, hearts entwined,
To the glimmering secrets of the cold.

Voices in the Crystal Silence

A hush drapes over the frozen land,
Whispers drift with the falling snow,
In the stillness, voices intertwine,
Songs of winter, soft and slow.

Every flake a note in the air,
Harmony fills the endless night,
Echoes through the crystal silence,
Chasing shadows with softest light.

Frosty breath mingles with the stars,
Each twinkle tells a tale untold,
In this symphony of winter's grasp,
Dreams are woven, bright and bold.

A nightingale's song breaks the calm,
Cradled in the snow's embrace,
Nature hums, a tender lull,
Life within this frozen space.

In the silence, we find our peace,
Resting under starry skies,
Voices echo all around,
In the crystal silence, we rise.

The Lament of the Snowbound

Winds howl like a lost refrain,
Drifting shadows play with fears,
Cloaked in white, the world feels still,
Yet beneath, the heart sheds tears.

Snowflakes whisper tales of loss,
Carried on the icy breath,
Each flurry a piece of forgotten dreams,
Wrapped in winter's coldest death.

In the depths of this biting chill,
Voices echo, soft and sweet,
Lamenting beneath heavy coats,
As icy chains hold fast their feet.

Branches creak and groan with age,
The sorrow of seasons long past,
In their silence, stories remain,
Of lives intertwined, forever cast.

Yet through the tears of the snowbound,
A glimmer of hope begins to glow,
For spring will break this frozen shroud,
And with it, the lament will go.

Milton Keynes UK
Ingram Content Group UK Ltd.
UKHW010228111224
452348UK00011B/580